The Sweet Lie
of
Lesbianism

*... the deception I thought
would make me happy.*

The Sweet Lie of Lesbianism

*... the deception
I thought would
make me happy.*

Sharon A. Lawson

Laurus BOOKS

The Sweet Lie
of
Lesbianism

... the deception I thought would make me happy.

By Sharon A. Lawson

Laurus Books
Post Office Box 2464
McDonough, Georgia 30253 USA
www.TheLaurusCompany.com

This book may be purchased from TheLaurusCompany.com, Amazon.com, and other retailers around the world.

*For a Searching Soul
who persistently posed the question to me:
"If my partner and I are both born again
Christians, and we deeply love one another
and are ready to make a commitment for life,
what can possibly be wrong with that?"
This book came from my pursuit of
God for His answer.*

ACKNOWLEDGEMENTS

ACKNOWLEDGEMENTS

Our Father has hand-picked these special intimate friends who have, over the years, dragged me back, sometimes kicking and screaming, when I foolishly considered returning to the old deceptions: Scott Erickson, Betty Faulk, Harold and Jan Huddleston (in whose singles' class I was born again), Sadie Johnson, Sharon Mayo, Mary N, and my precious sister, Janice Tullos. And Barbara Harris has showered me with the physical affection and the richly nurturing love of Jesus for which my soul had ached for so many years. There are countless others who have prayed for me since before I was in high school. My heart's deepest gratitude is poured out to God for each of you.

Our Father has also introduced these men of sensitivity and integrity into my life, some married and some single, who have chipped away at my old negative prejudices toward men that began to creep in when I was about twelve years old: Gary Blanton, Michael Carrigan, Scott Erickson, Dwain Johnston, Jim McLachlan, Alan Toles, and Tim Tyler. None of you can possibly imagine the impact you have had.

Not to remain unmentioned is my incredible pastor, Ron Hogue, whose life has been exemplary as a husband, father, writer, researcher, teacher, missionary at home and abroad, pastor to pastors, and above all, a diligent listener for the voice of the Holy Spirit. No one will realize until we get Home how many times you have spoken from the pulpit the exact words I needed to hear on that exact occasion for the issues with which I was struggling. So many times the course of my life has been altered or refined because of something the Father spoke directly to me through your words. I praise God for you and request that He reward you extravagantly on my behalf.

And last, but certainly not the least, is my publisher, Nancy E. Williams of The Laurus Company. She has been God's gift to me, not only with her publishing expertise, but in the jewels she has shared from her personal spiritual life that have inspired and encouraged me. This assignment from the Father could never have been completed nor found its way to any bookstore without your invaluable role in bringing it all together. I am so deeply grateful to Him for sharing you with me.

TABLE OF CONTENTS

TABLE OF CONTENTS

INTRODUCTION

INTRODUCTION

Although this book is written especially for a limited readership, born again lesbians who desire freedom from a disappointing lifestyle, there are many of us. If you are not among those who have been drawn to the seeming sweetness of lesbianism as the solution for your pain, you will not understand the strength of its hold on a wounded individual. It becomes a soul addiction—far more powerful than the physical addictions to nicotine, alcohol, or drugs—whose grasp is greatly intensified if you have ever actually been in love with one of your partners.

If you have been drawn into lesbianism but have not been born again, you will not likely understand its deception nor feel any need to break free from its deadly sweetness. Please know that I would never presume to hold any one of you accountable to me, only to your magnificent Creator who unconditionally and relentlessly loves you and desires to protect you and set you free. Someone once said, "I would rather live my life as if the Bible were true and die to find out it isn't, than live my life as if it isn't true and die to find out it is." Something worth considering.

Many, many years ago, just shortly after I became a born again Christian, the Holy Spirit called my attention to a particular Bible verse I had never noticed before and applied it personally to my own life. It read, "… And who knows but that you have come to the kingdom for such a time as this and for this very occasion."[1] I knew it was a reference to God's desire to use my former involvement in the gay community for His purposes, but I did not then have the experience with Him nor the uncompromised commitment to Jesus to talk about that. Now that the mass media is giving such extensive and positive coverage to gay rights and gay marriage, it is the time for me to share the story for which I was called into the kingdom.

When I was a very naive twelve year old, a slightly older relative molested me. It didn't go far enough to prematurely awaken my sexuality, but it implanted a great fear of men, knowing as I did that something was very wrong. Because he had cautioned me not to mention that incident to my mom, and because the several incidents that would follow occurred in the actual presence of my grandmother, it was well over a year before I finally summoned enough courage to tell my mother. She did not defend me. She did not comfort me. She did nothing to counter the implication that I was worth very little. She simply said, "It's no big deal. That's just the way men are."

They are? Really? They're all going to force me with their greater strength to do things I don't want to do?

They're all going to treat me as though what I want is irrelevant? She was my mom, and I believed her words. My silent response to her was, "In that case, I don't want one!" It was the first lie that pointed me toward lesbianism before I had ever even heard the word.

For a college acquaintance, the abuse started simply as what appeared to be innocent enough affection. When she was only five years old, her stepfather began grooming her to be flirtatious by manipulating her desire to please him; he gave her the affection she had longed for since her own daddy had left the family. It accelerated quickly to actual nightly rape before her childish mind could distinguish that anything was wrong. Her mom worked all night, and the other kids were sleeping, so it continued for three years (during which time she began to suspect something was not right about these activities) before she could ever tell another person what was happening. Because affection and sexuality became enmeshed in her mind, she's still uneasy with physical affection today unless it comes from a safe family member or a lesbian lover.

A co-worker who had been adopted as an infant had always wanted to find her birth mother and to know why she had not been valuable enough to keep. Her adoptive mom, however, was thrilled with the arrival of this new baby and, until her death, kept the letter describing the little one who would soon belong to her. And during her entire childhood, she was always her daddy's little darling. Somewhere in this seemingly idyllic childhood, there was a family friend, a man much respected in her small town community, who molested or raped her—even now, she won't share any details—and implanted a terror that still arises on the very rare occasions when his name comes up. In her early twenties, however, she even married a guy. Three weeks later, he decided she wasn't what he wanted. He threw her out but kept all the wedding gifts from her friends. Not long afterward, she slipped into seeking comfort within a lesbian relationship, and then another, and another.

A friend from summer camp had absolutely adored her daddy and bragged to all her friends about his many rugged accomplishments out in the oil fields. Then he'd had the nerve to abandon her by dying while she was only in junior high school. Her desperate mom had opened their home to an aunt and uncle who were never very fond of the young daughter. She soon came to despise this aunt who had begun to dominate her own home and was constantly criticizing her. She began to anticipate the comfort of sleepovers where experimentation with lesbianism began to offer some sweet relief from the dreaded return to a now comfortless house. When she left that home and went to college, there was a whole lesbian community waiting to welcome and embrace her.

We may have slipped into the lie under differing circumstances, they and you and I. Some of us were looking for something we desperately needed but never found, while others of us were attempting to replace something we greatly valued and lost, but the result was the same: lesbianism seemed like a sweet, comfortable choice for us. The little girl within each of us was still aching for the nurturing and affirmation she had always needed; she was probably looking for Mom.

Lesbianism looked like a great answer to the dilemma

of our souls, so we simply, imperceptibly absorbed some of the lies upon which it depends … until we got born again. And then the terrible incompatibility began to rage, didn't it? There seemed to be a gaping chasm between the precepts of the Bible and the lesbian agenda, an agenda that seemed to promise a happiness that had so long eluded us. Others within the church who had never experienced the same temptations as ours made us feel like inferior, second-class Christians.

Would you be willing to reexamine with a fellow Christian, one who long walked where you have walked, some of the deceptions upon which lesbianism depends?

As I examine certain of those lies, some of what I have included is "logos," conclusions that could easily have been drawn simply by a textual consideration and application of God's written Word, and some of it is definitely "rhema," concepts in which God has spoken His thoughts as a living conversation to me personally.

THE LIES

LIE #1: I was born that way.

*"I have been attracted to women all of my
life, or at least from as early as I can
remember, and I'm sure I was just born with
that particular leaning toward lesbianism."*

Could we look at that preference for a moment? Was it actually a sexual attraction, or was it an emotional preference for female company?

I've been drawn to women from the time I started first grade and began to make social connections with other people. I would like to suggest to you that my preference was simply the little child in me longing for the nurturing I had missed at home. That kind of nurturing is generally more readily available in women than in men.

Is that perhaps what you were searching for?

I simply wanted someone who loved me to put her arm around my shoulders and hug me. It started long before I had any concept of sexuality. I am now persuaded that for all of us, lesbianism had its roots somewhere in our early childhood: in traumas that occurred there; in terrible offenses we didn't realize we needed to forgive; or perhaps simply in deep, legitimate emotional needs that were not met adequately.

Many of us can even recall an early period of time when we believed that lesbianism was wrong, and we would not ever have considered getting involved in it. I remember once telling a lesbian friend that I was simply looking for a satisfying close relationship, not a lover, and she told me that I would certainly not find that within the lesbian community. She was right. Before much more time had elapsed, I made the choice to "buy" with sex the accompanying emotional closeness and physical affection I really wanted.

After a while, those encounters, referred to by some as "recreational sex," got to be fun, even though I never found in them any genuinely satisfying love, much less anyone with whom I wanted to spend my life. I did, however, begin to develop a sense of self-worth based on an established reputation for being good in bed. That was all that made me valuable. During those years, I probably would not even have known how to recognize the kind of love for which I was searching.

For others of us, it did begin as a sexual desire when some older person had used us to satiate their own sexual urges. At that point, the desire had been prematurely implanted in us, even before we were mature enough to be able to understand what had happened. And, in many cases, that abuse was the origin of an exceptionally intense sex drive that often led to experiences we weren't seeking and really didn't want at the same time that we were curious and drawn to them ... little children enticed into playing grown-up games ... adults earning for themselves a millstone around the neck in a deep sea grave![1]

At some point, the line between long-standing emotional need and sexuality got blurred, and it became easy to simply accept the fact that I must have been "born this way." There was abundant literature to confirm that as fact, and the more I read, the more convinced I became.

Do you recall the biblical statement that "Faith [or believing] comes from hearing, and hearing by the word of Christ"[2] and the biblical injunction to "Keep [guard] thy heart with all diligence; for out of it are the issues of life"[3]? Every "issue" (in Hebrew, "boundary") of significance is decided in the heart, or the mind, will, and emotions. I am now persuaded that whatever we believe, biblical or not, is a result of hearing and hearing, or reading and reading. We must protect our hearts from what gets imbedded there by being very selective in what we read or listen to. It has the potential to influence or shape what we have preferred to accept as truth. As I began to repress Biblical Truth for my own purposes and readily assumed that I was born with this "bent" toward lesbianism, I began to read that there was actual scientific research proving that some people were just born to be gay.[4] See there! I knew it!

However, upon further study, I found that the primary "research" was done by an openly gay man who had an agenda from the onset, and his "evidence" was "exaggerated and misleading."[5] From studying various cadavers, he had determined that the brain size of male homosexuals was consistently smaller than that of straight males and that the brain size of lesbians was consistently larger than that of straight females. The implication drawn from this very limited study of only 35 subjects was that the homosexuals involved were intrinsically, biologically gay. However, there was no way to know of their brain sizes at birth. Was the brain size simply biological, or was it perhaps the result of lifestyle experiences? Was that "bent" toward homosexuality a result of genetics or of exposure and choices made? Was there even a legitimate link between brain size at the end of life and one's sexual orientation?

Even a recent American Psychological Association publication, "Answers to Your Questions for a Better Understanding of Sexual Orientation & Homosexuality," includes an admission that there is no homosexual "gene"—meaning it is not likely that homosexuals are born that way—in contrast to APA's own statement in 1998 that "There is considerable recent evidence to suggest that biology, including genetic or inborn hormonal factors, play a significant role in a person's sexuality."

Peter LaBarbera, head of Americans for Truth About Homosexuality, believes the more recent statement is an important admission because it undermines a popular theory. "People need to understand that the 'gay gene' theory has been one of the biggest propaganda boons of the homosexual movement over the last 10 [or] 15 years," he points out. "Studies show that if people think that people are born homosexual they're much less likely to resist the gay agenda."[6]

Soon God began to deal with me personally about the issues of my biological nature, my lack of boundaries, and the 30+ years of determining what I liked, i.e., the choices I had made in my thought life as well as in actuality.

After reading the scripture that lists homosexuals among those who have no part in the kingdom of God,[7] the Father had me look at each category on that list: fornicator, idolater, adulterer, homosexual, thief, coveter, drunkard, reviler, swindler. None of those are inborn, and He pointed out that *all* of them are descriptions regarding what a person *chooses to DO* and can, therefore, *choose not to do*.

If one has a single adulterous affair, is that person an adulterer by birth? If one often gets drunk while attending college functions, is that person doomed by his biological makeup to be an alcoholic for life? Must a person who has a juvenile record for petty theft remain a thief forever? Those are all actions, and God reminded me of the lessons I had taught as a junior high school teacher about the difference between action verbs and linking verbs, between doing and being.

His rhema Word to me was: "Lesbianism is not who you ARE but what you (choose to) DO."

My wise pastor made that even more clear for me with his assertion that "Behavior is the clothing of identity,"[8] some of which clothing the Bible instructs us to "put off" or "lay aside."[9]

Just as I chose to take up lesbianism as a lifestyle that I thought would fulfill my needs, I have now chosen to lay it aside. At first, it was an extremely difficult choice, and it was made over a period of years with much intervention on the part of my heavenly Father; but there was no neurology, no genetics, no DNA involved.

LIE #2: I am intelligent enough to decide.

*"I am intelligent enough to know what I want,
what is good for me and another person, and
what self-determined agenda will make us
happy without requiring God's input."*

We all assume that we are intelligent enough to manage our own life choices because responsible independence is the American way, right? I suspect that the greater a person's I.Q., the greater is his/her vulnerability to this lie.

The truth, however, is that God is incomparably more intelligent, resourceful, and wise than the best of us. A god whose input is not vastly superior to mine, and perhaps incomprehensible to me, does not qualify to be God at all!

Whenever we prohibit God's input into our lives, we do so at great peril to ourselves! He even tries to warn us of that great danger when He says that having allowed the Word to slip from first place and final authority in my daily experience, I have repressed the Truth for my own purposes and made it inoperative in my life because I professed myself to be smart and got caught up in my own foolish

31

reasoning.[1] My personal safety absolutely depends upon my staying anchored in the Bible and submitting all my choices to the guidance my Father has provided in this love letter to His daughter. So why is *knowing* this so much easier than *doing* it?

I propose to you that this occurs because we do not really know, are not intimately acquainted with, the Father nor His Son, Jesus. It took me many years after I was genuinely born again and very familiar with the Bible to realize that I did not have the available and necessary intimacy with its Author.

A person with unconditional love for me earns the right to speak freely into my life, to tell me when he or she perceives some danger I might have overlooked, or some blind spot in my character that is causing problems for me. A person with whom I have only a surface acquaintance has not earned that right. Even if he or she does make some valid observation, if it is not based in an unconditional love for me, I probably will not give those remarks much serious attention. It is the same way with God.

I can clearly remember a period of time when I thought He was just out to "spoil my fun." Even after becoming a Christian, I didn't trust Him enough to allow Him to have much input into my daily decisions. Oh, I trusted Him enough to deliver me from the domain of the enemy, as far as I perceived it, but I wasn't ready to give Him complete charge of my life.

In that reservation, I was refusing to honor Him as God and was placing myself in charge.[2] Whoever is in charge has, for all practical purposes, now taken the place of God.

God showed me that thinking of myself as being wiser

than He is and, therefore, capable of determining what would best meet my deep emotional needs was the key element, the one thing that had to be in place in order for me to succumb to the appeal of lesbianism.[3]

I did not recognize that decision as blatant rebellion and idolatry, which like the sin of witchcraft brings us, perhaps unknowingly, under the enemy's authority.[4] The stage was set for the strategies of the Liar. Although his ways still seemed attractive to me, I did not know it would have such catastrophic effects in my life.

God says it twice, so He must have wanted to be sure I noticed it: "There is a way which seems right to a man [or woman], but its end is the way of death."[5]

For many years, I could have been defined as one of those living dead who had accepted Jesus as Savior but had definitely not yet surrendered my will to Him as my Lord. I had not then realized that I belong to the Smart One, and for my own peace and protection, I need to be under HIS control. Today, it is my greatest privilege and honor to know that He has been willing to take charge of every detail of my life.

LIE #3: I will not experience any consequences.

*"There will not be any consequences of a
lesbian sexual union when it occurs with
another consenting adult, especially when it
occurs within a lifetime commitment
to 'marriage.' "*

Thinking there will be no consequences may be what our current liberal society claims, but it doesn't work very well, even for non-believers, unless they are completely in denial. It works even less for those who have become born again.

So let's discuss consequences for a moment. What are they anyway?

It's important to know that consequences are **not** God's punishment for sin. Remember that sin is simply a person's choice to turn aside from Him to go her own way.[1] In the Old Testament, God did severely punish sin, but in the New Testament, the full punishment for sin has been laid on Jesus Christ in our place.[2] The Jewish people, as well as many other early civilizations, operated on the principle that without the shedding of blood, there is no forgiveness of sin.[3] Jesus fulfilled that requirement for us.

Under this New Covenant, which came into effect after Calvary, the Father now looks at us as righteous[4] and has chosen to rebuke and correct His children in one way alone—by His Word.[5]

So does that imply that we are now free to do whatever we desire without the fear of punishment? Without fear of punishment from God, yes; without fear of consequences, no. The difference in punishment and consequences is in their origin.

God is a good Father who always desires to provide for and protect those who belong to Him. But when we, by our own foolish choices, move out from under the safety of His protection, we move into the realm of the one who desires to destroy us. Jesus made the comparison when He said that He had come to give abundance to our lives but that there is an enemy who has come to steal and kill and destroy.[6]

Here's an example that helps me to grasp that vital difference in the origin of consequences.

The son of a wealthy doctor has everything he needs in his father's house—plenty of nutritious food, the finest clothing, and even physical health, but he decides to hang out in the slums with the homeless for a while where the water is polluted and there have been outbreaks of disease. When he becomes violently ill, is it punishment from his father for his having left home? No, it is simply the natural result, or consequence, of his having exposed himself to an unsafe environment.

When we step out from under the covering umbrella of our Father's Word and expose ourselves to the realm of an enemy, whether known to us or not, the results are just as predictable.

A discussion of consequences is a discussion of results, not punishments.

With that in mind, will you investigate with me what the Father tells us in His Word about the consequences of sin, especially sexual sin, to our bodies, our souls, and our spirits?

Bodily Consequences

The Word is very clear that *any* sexual relationship outside of marriage will have consequences that affect the body because that is a sin that occurs within and is directed against one's own body.[7] Several references more specific to homosexuality say that it causes one to reap the "inevitable consequences and penalty" within one's own body and personality[8] and that it will also accelerate to include being overtaken by a number of other offenses.[9]

In the overtly permissive society in which we live today, a person who is set on pursuing her own agenda can easily find rationalizations that these "worn arguments and old attitudes"[10] toward scriptural injunctions no longer apply. What she will *not* find, except within God's Word, is the encouragement to protect her heart from such attractive enticements, enticements that have consequences attached.

The Word of God instructs us that making our bodies a living sacrifice to Him is our only reasonable and required service,[11] but that does *not* suggest that our Father is a manipulative heavenly tyrant. Rather, we have that injunction for protection from our adversary who is constantly on the prowl, looking for someone who is vulnerable enough for him to devour.[12]

Bodily consequences almost always involve disease, and

I would like to detour momentarily from our topic in order to share with you some subjective applications of that topic from my own experience.

Shortly after my final lesbian involvement, I developed cancer for the first time (Hodgkin Lymphoma, 1996) as well as a diabetic side effect known as Charcot foot. After chemotherapy and radiation, I recovered from the cancer, but my foot remained incapable of bearing weight.

Still confused about the difference between punishment and consequences, I was furious at God. Hadn't I made a very difficult commitment to Him to leave and permanently shut the door on lesbian involvements? So why was I now being punished for the attractive indulgences I had rather grudgingly surrendered?

One clue that should have been obvious to me, but did not register with my conscious mind for many years, was the vulnerability of my unguarded heart. I had not recognized that I was still clutching the remote possibility that I might still return at some future time to the sweet relief from my pain that lesbianism had seemed to offer. I had no interest in again becoming involved in the old lifestyle or in the gay community, but I would have reconsidered the possibility of sexual intimacy with the one soulmate whom I had always loved.

May I insert at this point the fact that you cannot "con" the Father or the enemy. When you are obedient on the outside but still digging in your heels on the inside, both of them know how much of your heart belongs to each of them. That dualism of heart carries a threat that the enemy will begin to dilute, or weaken, your relationship with Jesus. It also carries the threat that the enemy will begin to show up at the most inopportune times in territory that still belongs to him.

A full nine years after I had removed myself, sexually and socially, from any lesbian contacts, another physical problem developed, and at a particularly inconvenient time.

My longtime soulmate was coming for a visit, and although we had been in touch over the intervening time span, we had not seen one another for a great many years. We both had been involved in lesbianism for about the same periods of time in our lives, although never together, and we both had been celibate for about the same more recent nine years.

Because we share an unusually intense relationship, and because we had the same background of lesbian experience, we approached our reunion with sincere caution and much prayer. God honored those prayers, and as it turned out, we were safe from any temptation for the entire length of almost constant companionship. That is not to imply, however, that I was completely single-minded. I still found myself very much attracted to her. I also failed to perceive any connection between that attraction and the simultaneously occurring physical problem.

Several days before the onset of this visit that I was approaching with double-mindedness, I noticed a lump on my leg that continued to grow to the size of a golf ball until it finally burst and began to drain a foul exudate. After another several months during which time it had still failed to dry up, I had it cultured. It was found to contain MRSA, that highly resistant staph infection. For another several years, interspersed with ineffective prescriptions for strong antibiotics, the infection persisted.

During the period of both these physical maladies, I had continued to talk to the Father about them, reminding Him of what an obedient daughter I had become … at least on the outside … and asking Him why He still felt the need to punish me. The enemy, who was the real culprit and knew where my heart remained, must have found an evil delight in those ignorant false accusations toward my Father who was continuing to love and protect me. The problem was that I was either not listening very carefully when He responded to me, or I was not giving very serious attention to the things that had come from Him because I was not absolutely sure they had.

One morning after some genuinely serious praying, the Father brought my attention to the already familiar story of Elijah and his dealings with the Israelites who had continued to forsake God and drift into the worship of idols.[13] Just prior to God's miraculous display of Himself in sending the fire that completely consumed their sacrifices, as well as the wet wood on their altar, Elijah had asked the people, "How long halt ye between two opinions? If the LORD be God, follow Him …"[14] Do you know what the literal translation of the word "halt" is? It is "limp."[15] How long will you *limp* between two opinions?

The implication should have been obvious to me, but it was not. Even though my physical body was limping, I could not understand how God could think I was still vacillating between two positions when I had been so compliant. I honestly wasn't aware that I was still clinging to lesbianism in my heart. So my thoughts defaulted to the natural, medical explanation: *it's just a side effect of the diabetes from which I had been told I could never expect to be free.*

Another morning while I was changing the repulsive dressing over that infection, I clearly heard the Father ask, "Do you think resistant staph is able to resist My Word or the Name of Jesus?" Of course, I didn't, so I continued to pray, always in the name of Jesus, and to focus on the Scriptures that promised healing.

During this period of time, the occasional thought would pass through my mind, "There is an infection in your soul, and it is lesbianism." Significantly, both the infection and the remaining attachment to lesbianism were hidden. The infection had not responded to antibiotics because it was lodged between some hardware and the bone, where circulation was not able to reach it; surgery was required to clean it all out. The lesbianism still hidden in my heart was just as difficult to remove and required some spiritual cleansing.

I had dismissed the above thoughts as irrelevant and not having originated with God because I had been celibate for such a very long time. My Father was responding to me, but the hidden allegiance in my heart kept me from applying what He was saying. I defaulted to the natural medical explanation again: *diabetics always have a difficult time fighting infection.*

In no way do I want to imply by the above accounts that I believe all sickness is caused by sin. I do not. But there is a stated biblical link between the turning aside into one's own selfish agenda and its physical consequences. I am inclined to think that whatever is going on within the heart, or soul, of an individual tends to manifest itself in the flesh.[16] There is even scientific evidence of that link in certain diseases.

Soul Consequences

A second consequence of sexual sin is the establishment of soul ties, the emotional and mental ties that bind a couple together. These ties are a great advantage within the purity of a marriage, but have dire consequences outside of marriage.

When God says that we become one whenever we have a sexual encounter with another person, that oneness is not simply the obvious physical.[17] Our soul—the mind, will, and emotions—becomes interwoven with the mind, will, and emotions of that other person, and that connection is not broken in the soul whenever the physical connection is interrupted.

A soul tie is a wondrous plan the Father devised to add stability and permanence to a marriage—one man and one woman for life—or to a nonsexual relationship He has ordained for His purposes. But when that soul tie occurs between two people who do not remain committed, or who perhaps never intended any commitment, it contaminates future relationships. When there have been many such sexual unions, and therefore many soul ties as well, one individual becomes permanently connected, handcuffed if you will, to many different partners.

Have you ever met a divorced person who sincerely wanted to move on with life and be faithful to the current spouse but still experienced frustratingly strong ties to a former spouse? Have you ever met a single person who just could not seem to make a permanent commitment, who did not seem to be able to get his/her act together enough to focus on the needs of a current dating partner? In many cases, this occurs because there are still strong soul ties in effect that create a divided emotional loyalty or a sense of scattered identity because they don't know who or whose they are.

Soul ties are great for marriage when they only occur the one time, but soul ties can wreak havoc when they come about as a result of recreational or transitory sex with more than one partner.

Spiritual Consequences

A final consequence of lesbianism, as with any sin, is the spiritual separation from a living, interactive relationship with God.

It is to that consequence I believe the Bible is referring when it says that homosexuals, and others on that afore-mentioned list, will not inherit the kingdom of God.[18]

Because scripture says that the kingdom of God is within us,[19] I do not believe the above reference is a reference to the final destination of heaven. It is, rather, to the availability of a quality of life here in the earth where God is Ruler.

That "kingdom" is one in which we submit ourselves to God's authority and interact with Him in His earthly business with us as kingdom residents.

Of course, there will not be anyone in heaven involved in fornication, idolatry, adultery, homosexuality, theft, covetousness, drunkenness, reviling, or swindling, but you may be sure there will be many there who, having been washed clean by the blood of Jesus before or afterward, will have done these things while they were here in the earth. And they will not have been denied entrance to heaven because of it.

That will be the topic of our next discussion.

LIE #4: I can be Christian and lesbian.

*"I can still be a born again Christian while I am
involved in a lesbian relationship or
maintaining my lesbian identity."*

Technically, you are born again if you have accepted the blood payment of Jesus for your sin debt, but you will not be able to live an effective Christian life and remain lesbian because your heart cannot actually belong to two people at the same time.

Becoming a Christian is a matter of accepting Jesus Christ as my Savior, as the One who completely paid the penalty for my sins by shedding His blood so that I could stand guiltless before God. I can accept His redemptive gift and remain in a lesbian relationship … but only briefly.

I tried to make the two converge, but ultimately, it just would not work. I was having difficulty with the guilt that was pressing in on me. I felt like my prayers were not getting past the ceiling of the bedroom.

About that time, God showed me: "Behold, the Lord's hand is not shortened at all, that it cannot save, nor His ear dull with deafness, that it cannot hear. But your iniquities [an interesting word that means one's "bent," "twistedness," or "inclination toward sin"] have made a separation between you and your God, and your sins ["turning aside from God to your own agenda"[1]] have hidden His face from you, so that He will not hear."[2]

Besides being freed from the penalty of sin (selfish pursuits), becoming a Christian was also a matter of exchanging my own life for His, of making the choice to receive him as Lord, CEO, in charge of all the decisions I would henceforth be making.

I tried really hard to make my preferences nobody else's business, but when you have honestly surrendered your life to Jesus and actually allowed Him to take up residence in your heart, it becomes His business. He says that "No man can serve two masters: for either he will hate the one, and love the other; or else he will hold to the one, and despise the other …"[3] In order to be committed to lesbianism, a Christian has to push Jesus into the far recesses of her mind, and typically, He will not remain there.

Where there is a lie, there is the Liar. The one who has told you those sweet lies about lesbianism is not at all threatened if you want to join a church. You can even host a women's Bible class, organize the singles' retreat, or lead the praise and worship team and come away from it looking pretty righteous, if you aren't openly sexually active or flaunting your lesbian orientation.

As Christians, however, we no longer have the right to our own preafrence—what we prefer to think is right. We must now live by principle—what the Father tells us in His Word is right. The only thing that enables us to do that, or even makes us *want* to, is knowing Him personally and intimately. He says that HE is at work within us, causing us to want what He wants and enabling us to do what pleases Him.[4] Originally, I knew I did not want what He wanted, but an unexpected change in my attitude began to evolve after I chose to obey Him anyway. He says that when I commit my ways—those things I choose to DO—to Him, He then establishes my thoughts, begins to stabilize my wrong thinking, and brings my attitudes into agreement with His.[5] I saw that I had the easier part, and He would do the harder part.

The essential question then becomes "Who has my heart?" and both the Father and the enemy are equally aware of the answer. For me personally there came a curiously accurate indicator of that answer. It was the declining function of my long standing "gaydar," that uncanny ability that is almost universally present among gays to recognize even a stranger's gay orientation. That capacity is not the sensitive discernment of a kindred soul that most gays would like to believe it is, but rather it is the presence of two deceptive evil spirits, one clinging to each individual, acknowledging one another in the spirit realm. It is one of the enemy's chief means of targeting potentially vulnerable persons in this joint demonic assignment to bring them together. If your gaydar still alerts you to the presence of another potential lesbian connection, it is advantageous to protect your heart by making a hasty departure.

Trusting Jesus enough to fully surrender my heart to Him has been a lifelong process, and for some of us that process has come easier than for others. For me, it took a giant leap forward when I began to present to Him daily needs that were too big for me to handle. I was greatly relieved to find Him so willing to involve Himself in performing (accomplishing, finishing, and perfecting) those things that concerned me.[6]

Can you grasp with me the magnitude of the fact that the Creator and King of the universe would notice and make time to involve Himself in whether or not I could get my car's electric windows up when rain was expected, or whether it had air-conditioning when the temperature outside was 104 degrees, or whether I had laundry money when all my clothes were dirty? None of those things presents a life-altering situation, but He cares about them and involves Himself in them because He cares about me. He began to consistently show Himself more than adequate for every specific need as I would bring those to Him.

As my trusting dependence upon Jesus began to grow, the enemy also used that point in time to aggressively demonstrate the claim he still had to my life. I had done nothing to get rid of those former desires because I seldom thought about them; they had remained far back in the recesses of my mind where I would never have acted upon them, but they were still there nonetheless.

Neither had I identified how much those former desires contradicted my increasingly satisfying relationship with Jesus, nor how very threatening to my relationship with Him they could potentially become. But the Liar was well aware of their presence and their usefulness to him.

I had been celibate for many years by this time in my spiritual growth and was becoming more intimately acquainted with Jesus, not just with what He had done or said long ago. I was beginning to experience a peaceful interrelationship with Him and His purposes for me. But suddenly old ways that I had long ago abandoned began to spring to mind with unusual frequency. Fantasy thoughts would come to me, and because lesbianism still had a corner of my heart, I did not refute them but passively indulged in considering them. I began to dwell on the seductive appeal of former conversations, flirtatious suggestions, memories, and activities of long ago.

I had begun to notice a strong pull back toward the old lifestyle and wondered what it might be like to revisit the old bars. WHOA!! I would never actually go to those empty places that no longer had anything to offer me. That just wasn't who I had become.

I still did not pay much attention to what was happening, however, until I began to have recurring thoughts of exploring Internet lesbian pornography. That was a huge "red flag." I had never visited those sites in the past, and I recognized the presence of someone or something that was definitely "not me."

That was another unmistakable clue that I needed to confront the Liar behind those sweet lies that had always promised what they had never delivered.

Suddenly that deception presented a serious threat to all God had accomplished in me. I think that was the first time I had ever been able to look at lesbianism as the Father does, as something inherently evil, something destructive, something from which He had long wanted to protect me. For the first time since I was about twelve years old, Jesus' statement that He is the Truth that would set me free[7] began to be activated in that very deceived area of my life.

LIE #5: I can choose without impacting others.

"Since I am in charge of my own life, my personal intimate choices do not affect other people, and therefore, if my having sex with another consenting adult is acceptable to us, it is nobody else's business."

In addition to the sexual abuse from a relative, there had been as late as high school some physical abuse under the guise of "discipline" from my father. I had vowed that after I was able to escape from his house, no man would ever again have that kind of power over me.

Having become rather frightened of men, or of anyone I could not control, I made myself readily available to the non-threatening gay and straight women I began to meet once I was away at college. In addition to the lie regarding independence, there was the lie that I needed to become self-protective because, at that time, I had no real working relationship with my Heavenly Father who wanted to protect me.

Everything changed when I became a Christian. Very abruptly, there arose a terribly uncomfortable clashing of values between the truth of God's Word and the lies of lesbianism, lies to which I had been clinging in order to survive. I soon found out that even my body was no longer my own, that it was the temple of the Living God, and that I had been bought (as a slave) with a price.[1]

I discovered that God's reasonable expectation was that I would now consider my body a living sacrifice, set apart to be used for His purposes[2] and that I who had been made the righteousness of God[3] was no longer to be yielding my members (parts of my body) as instruments of unrighteousness.[4]

God made the "rhema" application of those references particularly graphic for me. He reminded me that He wanted to use my mouth to teach and encourage, and to praise Him. He wanted to use my hands to comfort others and to impart His Spirit for healing. I had used them for quite different purposes. It embarrassed me to consider that He knew specifically about every lesbian activity in which I had participated! So much for independence and being able to choose a dual existence.

Once I became a Christian, I knew I could no longer live as if I were independent of God. Nor could I live as if I were disconnected from others in my decisions and actions. Those two lies are basic to the deceptive independence of lesbianism. They had given me the freedom to believe that what I chose to do in my private life would not significantly affect others. That is the way most of the non-Christian world lives, but it was never the Father's intention for His family of believers to live that way. He made us to be interrelated, to need the support of other people, to influence and to be influenced by those who are also connected to Him. He made us to be responsible, to a degree, for one another.

Joni Lamb quotes the Father in her book, *Surrender All*, as having said in a "rhema" word to her, "When we fail to surrender our own lives to our Creator, that too can have a profound negative effect on others who are destined to be connected to our purpose. When we lack faith or falter in our faith, it not only affects our own lives, it impacts all who fall within our sphere of influence."[5]

I thought of a beloved Christian friend who has an earnest desire for everyone she meets to know about Jesus. One day, she had spent a lengthy lunch time telling a non-believer about Him, but when the man expressed a desire to get more intimately acquainted with her, she withdrew by announcing that she is lesbian.

What does that communicate to those outside the faith, or within it? If we Christians are free to choose lesbianism, why would another person be prohibited from choosing an extra-marital affair with some cute guy at the office to whom she is attracted? And what of the younger ones among our own families, friends, and neighbors who are onlookers?

Young people today are not as naive as we once were, and they are quick to perceive what we may think we have hidden. If we espouse Christianity while embracing a lesbian lifestyle, or even a lesbian philosophy, what does that communicate to them about the validity of biblical values for their own lives?

We have lost the right we once thought was ours to live in independent isolation once we have committed ourselves to the Father's always interrelational agenda to represent Him to the world around us.

My commitment to Jesus was genuine, and late in my

final lesbian relationship, I had promised Him that if He would get me untangled from that mess, I would never go back into it. I haven't. What was there to draw me back to the disappointing instability and emptiness of the life I had left behind?

When He did get me out, I thought I had at last escaped the lure of that lifestyle, but seven years later, I began to reconsider the lie. It still had a tenacious hold on me because I had earlier committed to it as that which would assuage the terrible pain in my heart. I was still hurting. During that seven years, I had been abandoned by at least three straight Christian friends whom I had genuinely and purely loved.

The worst and the best were yet to come because Jesus says that the Liar will always return with reinforcements to a house (heart) that is swept clean but left empty of real intimacy with Himself.[6]

Fortunately, He also promises that no one will ever be able to snatch from out of His Father's hand those who are truly His.[7]

THE TRUTH

THE TRUTH:
Jesus can set me free from the lies.

"I am considering the possibility that I have believed a lie[1] that looks very desirable but is destructive for myself and others. However, my thought patterns remain essentially unchanged. What do I do now?"

To the born again Christian, freedom from the attraction and deception of the lesbian lie is readily available, and I want to share with you several specific ways to come into that freedom if you really want it.

The first is forgiveness. The Word of God tells us that if we refuse to forgive when we are angry, that will give a foothold or make a legal opportunity for the enemy to operate in our lives.[2] That does not suggest that those who have hurt us or damaged us or offended us will ever ask for or deserve our forgiveness. It simply gives us the information we need to shut a door of protection against the enemy's plans for us.

In his book, *Freedom through Forgiveness*[3], Nathan Daniel gives several accounts of homosexuals who were immediately set free from that lifetime lie simply by forgiving those who had caused horrible damage to them.

He also presents the practical process of mentally taking an offender to court, a process that has been extremely helpful to me in finding freedom from the many years of accumulated anger in my soul. Here's how that courtroom drama plays out:

I come to court as the Victim who is not particularly interested in forgiving her Offender, and I bring with me the Prosecuting Attorney, Satan, who is always the eternal accuser.[4] The Judge is Father God Who invites me to present my charges to Him. Once I have done that, He calls for some input from Jesus, the Defense Attorney, the eternal Advocate for the guilty.[5] Jesus recommends that the offender be forgiven because He has already paid the full price, the penalty, for that person's sin, whether or not the offender ever accepts that payment. He recommends grace, an undeserved favor from the court.

The Judge looks back at me and asks what I recommend that He do with my offender. Then He adds that whatever I recommend for my offender will be what He will also be obligated to do with me in response to my own sins.[6] "Shall I drop the charges against him, or judge him to the full extent of the law?"

Now I'm needing to rethink my case. That person really did hurt me in a way that has stolen years from my life, and he has never shown even the slightest hint of remorse. However, my own unforgiveness has contaminated my soul with anger and resentment for just as many years, and the Word tells me that my lack of forgiveness has also given opportunities for the enemy to harass me.[7] I have always been in desperate need of the Father's mercy, so I guess I had better ask Him to extend that same mercy to my enemy.

I ask Him to drop the case, and I agree to a threefold plan of restoration for my own soul, whether or not it ever affects my offender. I agree to FORGIVE him for what he has done, RELEASE him from the penalty of the judgments I have held against him, and BLESS him in the name of Jesus.

Now you may be sure that my real enemy, the prosecuting attorney, is mad as hell. And for a time, he is likely to keep reminding me of the terrible hurts from which I allowed my offender to escape punishment … just as Jesus allowed me to escape punishment. In those moments, I will have to renew my original decision. By an act of my will and for as long as it takes, I will choose over and over again to forgive, release, and bless the one who, like myself, was guilty and required the blood of Jesus.

Nathan Daniel's book helped me to see my need to forgive a number of people. There were more than 100 in all, from childhood through college to the present, some of whom I had entirely forgotten until the Holy Spirit spoke their names to me. The process of forgiveness continued for several days, but afterward I experienced a refreshing cleansing from the anger that had long been resident in my heart.

For many people caught up in the homosexual lifestyle, that forgiveness has brought complete release immediately. For me, there was something more I still needed to do.

I had opportunities to renounce lesbianism at any time after I accepted Jesus, and I would have saved myself much anguish had I done so. But it held a fascinating sweetness for me, and I was still drawn to its deception. Once that uncharacteristic and surprising acceleration of old thought patterns began emerging, I knew I was still in grave danger.

Have you ever noticed that when we finally become

genuinely ready to listen, Jesus is always ready to provide the answers we need? As He has often done for me when I was having any difficulty hearing Him, He spoke to me through another wise pastor's insightful message.

Ron Hogue has extensive experience in ministering to broken lives, and in one of his online Sunday sermons, he was teaching about the necessity of "Breaking Covenant with the Enemy,"[8] a message that would become life altering for me. He referred to the Old Testament account in which Joshua and his men had inadvertently made a binding covenant of peace with their enemies, the Gibeonites.[9]

The Old Testament contains types and shadows of modern day life, and this ancient story certainly mirrored my own situation accurately. Israel had been in a place of obedience, victory, and peace with their God at that time—just as I had been—and the Gibeonites had come to them disguised as strangers from a distant land who simply sought their protection. Although one of Joshua's men had questioned whether these strangers might indeed be enemies,[10] no one stopped to request God's counsel but proceeded to extend the covenant protection they had thought was all right. That soon put them in the position of having to defend those who wanted to destroy them.

I realized that I had long been in that position myself, as I had made peace with and coddled in my own mind the sweetness of what lesbianism had still seemed to offer me. That became uncomfortably apparent as I listened to Ron Hogue's definition of that covenant. He said, "A covenant of peace with the enemy is the agreement to accept the presence of something in our hearts that is hostile and contradictory to the will of Christ." Ouch!

The impact of that truth was astounding to me. Because I was genuinely born again, I knew I had an irrevocable covenant with Jesus Christ. What I had never considered, until that moment, was the possibility that I might simultaneously have had other covenants in effect. I thought my covenant with Jesus had automatically canceled out all others, but suddenly I recognized the truth of that duplicity in my heart. It explained why my increasingly closer relationship with Jesus had so stirred up those old thoughts. My relationship with Him was a terrible threat to the Liar's long-standing covenant with me.

I verbally renounced and broke that old covenant with lesbianism in the name of Jesus. It was easy, and when I did so, the results were immediate. From that incredible moment, I have lived in complete freedom from the lie of lesbianism. That is not to suggest that the enemy never proposes temptations, but I do not any longer consider them attractive. I have not once wanted to return there. Best of all, the love I have long had for my closest friend is now completely pure, no longer contaminated by any of the old attractions and desires. Now I can choose, without compromise, to honor Jesus with my life. I am FREE for the first time in many, many decades!

If you want to do so, you too can break that old covenant. It took effect with your first lesbian encounter and had permission to remain as long as you coddled the thought of lesbianism as the sweet solution for your pain. Has it ever delivered on its promises for more than just a brief interval? Has it increased its aggression as you have turned from it and become more intimately acquainted with Jesus? Or have you made the effort to become more intimately acquainted with Jesus?

The lie will never be as sweet as it once had promised to be, now that you have glimpsed the Truth. The Liar behind the lie of lesbianism, that ruthless destroyer, has been exposed. We belong to the One who is the eternal, living Love for which we had been searching in all the wrong places. I entrust each one of you to that incredible love of Jesus.

THE TRUTH: Freedom can be permanent.

*"If the Son therefore shall make you free, ye
shall be free indeed,"[1] but complete and
permanent freedom is a joint endeavor between
Jesus and me, which requires my committed
participation. What if I can't keep my part?*

Some time has passed now since I experienced that initial release from the longstanding covenant with lesbianism that spanned more than 30 years of my life, and it is always good to discover what will or will not stand the test of time. After 30 years of involvement in the lesbian community followed by fifteen years of celibacy, I can now assure you that the freedom Jesus Christ offers certainly can be permanent. It is not automatic, however. I am coming to believe that its permanence depends upon three critical factors.

First, you must completely surrender to Jesus and maintain an intimate relationship in which pleasing Him and bringing Him glory in everything you do is the priority of your life. Ask yourself: Who does my heart really belong to? Who does my body belong to? Is this a permanent, lifetime commitment? When you genuinely love Jesus and have committed yourself—body, soul, and spirit—to Him for the rest of your life, freedom is not a difficult thing. But if you are still more interested in what you want, the enemy will constantly tempt you with a vast array of attractive but deceptive choices.

As you remind yourself of the ultimate sacrifice Jesus made for you and all the specific things He has accomplished in your life since you were born again, your love for Him will grow. Keep on getting to know Him better, and keep on increasing the intimacy you have with Him. By the way, He will never push you into a heterosexual marriage; He has simply called you to be His.

Here is a delightful true story that will illustrate that process. My closest friend is the highly-intelligent recipient of a Ph.D., but she is terrified of spiders, no matter what kind or size. She is also a born-again Christian who is still butting heads with God over the lesbianism issue, and none of our discussions or my prayers for God to speak to her had seemed to alter that very much.

One day, some careless spider crawled out across her living room floor, and she went berserk, spraying insecticide all over the room until the place was seriously toxic. Her reasoning: there might be other spiders in the wall that could emerge later.

Then she spied a helpless little moth, a creature too closely related to the butterflies she adores to be ignored. She chased it all over that room, huffing and puffing as she inhaled the insecticide, grasping wildly but unsuccessfully at it with both hands so that she could carry it outside. Finally, stopping with her hands on her hips, she shouted at it, "How can I set you free if you won't let me catch you?"

In that stunning moment, the Father spoke to her more clearly than I ever could have done. Letting Him catch us is equivalent to trusting Him enough to completely surrender our own agendas to Him so that He can set us free from every toxic environment in which we find ourselves.

The second factor in maintaining your freedom is guarding your heart and mind.[2] That is where the lie originally got imbedded and reinforced. You must submit everything which influences you—what you are thinking, what you are feeling, what you are reading, what claims you are listening to another person make, who your closest friends are, and especially what our society's fluctuating mores suggest—to what the Father says to you in His Word. Is there agreement or conflict? If there is conflict, you cannot afford to consider the validity of those other influences because they are what originally contaminated your concept of Truth. You have to focus on the fact that the lesbian lie may look and sound sweet on the surface, but it is a lie nevertheless. You must remind yourself of its tremendous hidden threats to you and those you love.

Apart from continually immersing yourself in our Father's perspective, it is rather difficult to maintain that focus. That is the reason we are instructed to trust in the Lord with all our hearts, remembering that He is the Smart One Who plans the path that will most fulfill our lives. We are not to lean to our own understanding because our perception is immensely limited and vulnerable, and it is subject to a deception we have mistakenly believed would make us happy.[3]

So, yes, there is permanent freedom, and there is One Who will enable you to make the right choices to maintain it ... over and over again ... if you want it.

Even if you miss it and temporarily stray from His path for you, He will bring you back to that freedom. But let me tell you that it is much more difficult to break free from the deceiver once you have reconsidered his lies or have detoured from the path Jesus has for you.

There is a third factor that will strengthen you and enable you to remain on the path with Jesus, and that is involvement in a church family. God did not warn us against forsaking church on Sundays[4] because He is keeping a heavenly scorecard of our attendance. He knows how vulnerable we are and how much we need support and fellowship with like-minded believers. He knows we need some earthly accountability to keep us from being ambushed again by some sweet lie the enemy will still attempt to plant in our thoughts.

Really, we need people with whom we can be completely transparent. And He will give us those with whom we can share with absolute honesty without any fear of rejection. At first, there may be only one, or perhaps two, but as you become more deeply acquainted with the members of your church family, others will become more open. Their love for you will give you the sense of safety you need in order to become transparent with them. But, be wise enough at first to allow Jesus to choose these intimate friends and bring them to you. Sharing with those who have not yet learned the dangers of judging another person can become a reckless disaster for you. Been there!

Pursue Jesus. Reject every other conflicting, deceptive encroachment upon your mind and heart.

THE TRUTH: Bringing It All Together

"When I need comfort, I am now retraining myself. I will run to Jesus and talk with Him or run to His Word for encouragement. I will saturate my soul with music that draws me back to Him or spend time rejoicing in His truths with a beloved Christian friend. Is there anything else I need?"

During a hospital confinement, the Father taught me several things that seemed to bring some pieces of my puzzle together into a more meaningful whole. Once again, He emphasized to me the essential inter-relatedness of body and soul, wherein whatever happens in the one often reflects what is happening in the other.

Just as I was making some significant progress in being able to walk again, I was hospitalized because the MRSA (resistant staph infection) that I knew was in my leg was also found to be dormant in my foot, and it had become active again. Something a precious nurse shared with me that I had never known was the fact that the real culprit behind all my difficulties was sugar.

Sugar, which is known to suppress the immune system, will thus nurture any infection resident within the body, especially in a diabetic body. Because of a number of stresses then present in my life, I had been irresponsibly consuming "comfort foods," i.e., sugars, at a rate that had escaped my attention. It had happened several times over the years that just as I was experiencing a measure of healing in my foot, it would break down again. I simply could not understand what was happening.

Was my walking on it causing those breakdowns? Was God just teasing me with a measure of healing that I would never fully possess? Surely, He wouldn't do that, would He?

Then came the enlightenment: the problem had been with ME all along! God kept restoring health to me, and just as it was becoming manifest, I would allow my need for real comfort to result in a substitutionary sugar overload. He was continually healing me, and in my ignorance, I was continually destroying what He was giving.

What an embarrassing realization! But what potential for change it brought! I'm just like most of you: I very much enjoy chocolate and caramel and ice cream, but would I trade those things for my ability to walk? Absolutely not! Heartfelt, humble repentance was my immediate response to the Father who had always been faithful to me. I will now assume greater responsibility for myself!

You may be wondering, "What does this have to do with our consideration of lesbianism?" A LOT! I can't say that the implications were at first very clear to my lightning-fast mind, but God is such a patient Teacher with all of us.

Just as He had long been attempting to heal my body from the impact of sugar, He had long been attempting to heal my soul from the impact of lesbian involvement. For long periods of time, I would make appreciable strides toward what I knew He wanted. Then I would blow it again.

I never got sexually involved again, but there was the evil one who regularly taunted me with the seeming sweetness of the lie and who continually suggested to me that I was missing out on something really wonderful. And it is that consideration of the deceptive "sweetness" that keeps us from complete freedom.

Every fond memory, every flirtation ever returned, every suggestive thought breaks down our spiritual immune system. It makes the deceptive lie seem to be even sweeter, and it has been the enemy's relentless ruse to make something that is destructive, no matter what that something is, look desirable to us.

To allow my mind to go to those places in pursuit of comfort is the same as a diabetic's allowing herself to run to sugar in pursuit of comfort. The irony of sugar (for me) and the irony of lesbianism is the same: *the desire for its sweetness empowers a great hidden evil that is bent on destroying me.*

Both are deceivers, and both are destroyers. Both promise a comfort and sweetness they cannot genuinely deliver. But Jesus can. And that is the incredibly good news!

We sometimes take a tediously long time to discover the Truth that it is He who offers every fulfilling thing for which we have been looking.

So I have a responsibility now to protect what the Father has given me. I do not nearly as often run to sugar for emotional comfort because of the disastrous effects it has on my physical body, and I do not ever run to lesbianism for emotional comfort because its effects on my spirit are even more disastrous. As a result, I expect to be walking and running in the near future, and I am anticipating the most satisfying walk with Jesus that I have ever experienced as I assume responsibility for my own choices.

THE TRUTH:
What does it mean to be "born again"?

*"Jesus replied ... 'You should not be surprised
at my saying ... you must be born again.'"* [1]

To be "born again" means that I now truly belong to Someone else who loves me as I have always wanted and needed to be loved. It means that this unconditional love will not ever be withdrawn, even if I make some really bad choices. It means that whenever I need to talk about anything, that One is always available to listen and to get involved.

Jesus made the decision to give His life for me before He had any guarantee that I would respond. That offer is available to you as well. He poured out His blood as the full payment for all of my sins, and yours, and left it up to us to accept or refuse His offer. When I accepted His offer, I gave Him my own life in exchange for the life that He had given for me.

What does that mean now? It means that He is now the One in charge of every area of my life. It does not mean, however, that He has obliterated my free will. I can still go my own way and disobey Him … if I want to deal with the results, the consequences, of my actions.

But here is the absolutely incredibly wonderful part of this exchange. He, whose wisdom far exceeds the limitations of my own and the range of whose influence is incomparably greater than my own, promises that HE will accomplish, finish, and perfect whatever concerns me.[2] What a huge promise from a huge God! I can become like a little child now with no heavy worries or concerns. And I have found such a security in Him that I seldom ever worry about anything anymore. If I get distracted and lose sight of whose I am, He reminds me that I may cast all my cares over onto Him because He is caring for me.[3] I've got to tell you that this is the most peaceful and secure way to live that I have ever encountered.

Once recently, I had lost sight of whose I am and was focused on a very distressing situation that I was unable to resolve on my own. In tears, I cried out to Him, "I don't know what to do!" Immediately, I heard in my mind His gentle answer, "I do." "But Lord, I have nothing to bring to the resolution of this situation," I foolishly reminded Him. Then I heard Him say, "I will do it." That settled the matter for me. The Big One was at work on my little problem!

If becoming "born again" sounds like something you have needed, it is a very simple matter. You just pray and ask Jesus to come into your heart and take over your life. Then He does so. If you don't know what to say, You can use a prayer similar to this one:

"Lord Jesus, my life has become a disappointing mess, and I'm just not able to straighten things out. Please come into my heart and make me a new person. I receive Your blood as the full payment for all my sins, past, present, and future, completely washing them all away. I thank You for doing that for me, and I now invite You to be completely in charge of every area of my life from this day forward. Help me now to live for You as You have died for me. Amen."

Eventually, you will learn to hear Him speaking to you in your spirit, but in the meantime, you can always hear Him speaking to you in His Word. Begin the practice of reading the Holy Bible daily in a translation that you can understand.

Before I say "good-bye," I would like to share with you some resources that now nurture and safeguard my soul. I love you, precious ones … but not as much as Jesus does! See you at Home when we are finished here!   —Shar

ADDENDUM

ADDENDUM

SCRIPTURES (Italics mine)

There is a way that seems right to a man *[or woman]*, but in the end it leads to death.[1]

Claiming to be wise *(without consulting God)*, they became fools [professing to be smart, they made simpletons of themselves].[2]

Therefore:

Trust in the LORD with all your heart and do not lean on your own understanding. In all your ways acknowledge Him, and He will make your paths straight.[3]

MUSIC

The words to the following songs are very powerful and energizing to the soul. I so much want you to be able to see them, but copyrights forbid my including the lyrics here. However, if you have a computer, you should be able to see the words at the Internet sites I have included, and hopefully, you will be able to listen to them as well.

"I Will Change Your Name"[1]
from cassette album, *Live Worship Songs of the Vineyard, We Exalt Your Name #3, "Touching the Father's Heart."*
Audio: www.youtube.com/watch?v=HyhsSFT6A5k
Lyrics: www.worship.co.za/tfh/t03f0412.asp

"Mercy Said No"[2]
from CeCe Winans' CD, *Throne Room.*
Audio: www.youtube.com/watch?v=Z_SjhKJgqGg
Lyrics: www.sing365.com/music/lyric.nsf/Mercy-Said-No-lyrics-
    Cece-Winans/6389BB3D64EAEC4F48256DB000114D4D

"Hold Me Close"[3]
from Kim Hill's CD, *Arms of Mercy.*
Audio *(choose #3)*: www.rhapsody.com/kim-hill/arms-of-mercy
Lyrics: www.christianlyricsonline.com/artists/kim-hill/hold-
    me-close.html

REFERENCES

REFERENCES

Introduction

[1] Esther 4:14 AMP

LIE #1: I was born that way.

[1] Matthew 18:6

[2] Romans 10:17 NASB [brackets added]

[3] Proverb 4:23 KJV [brackets added]

[4] Simon LeVay, "A Difference in Hypothalamic Structure Between Heterosexual and Homosexual Men," *Science*, August 30, 1991, pp. 1034-37.

[5] Joe Dallas, *A Strong Delusion*, Harvest House Publishers, 1996, pp. 112-114.

[6] Charlie Butts in an online article, "APA revises 'gay gene' theory," for the American Family Association's *OneNewsNow*, May 14, 2009.

[7] 1 Corinthians 6:9-10 AMP

[8] Ron Hogue, New Heart Ministry, "Dismantling Behavioral Schemes," August 8, 2007

[9] Ephesians 4:22, Hebrews 12:1

LIE #2: I am intelligent enough to decide.

[1] Romans 1:21-22 AMP

[2] Romans1:21 AMP

[3] Romans 1:22-24 AMP

[4] 1 Samuel 15:23

[5] Proverbs 14:12, 16:25 NASB (brackets added)

LIE #3: I will not experience any consequences.

[1] Isaiah 53:6a
[2] Isaiah 53:6b
[3] Hebrews 9:22 NASB
[4] 2 Corinthians 5:21
[5] 2 Timothy 3:16
[6] John 10:10
[7] 1 Corinthians 6:18
[8] Rom. 1:27 AMP
[9] Rom.1:28-31 AMP
[10] President Barack Obama in his speech to homosexuals in the East Room of the White House on Monday, June 29, 2009
[11] Romans 12:1
[12] 1 Peter 5:8
[13] 1 Kings 18
[14] 1 Kings 18:21 KJV
[15] 1 Kings 18:21 AMP
[16] Psalm 31:10b, Psalm 32:3-5, Psalm 38:3, John 5:14, 1 Corinthians 5:1-5, James 5:15b
[17] 1 Corinthians 6:16-17
[18] 1 Corinthians 6:9-10
[19] Luke 17:21

LIE #4: I can be Christian and lesbian.

[1] Isaiah 53:6
[2] Isaiah 59:1-2 AMP [brackets added]
[3] Matthew 6:24
[4] Philippians 2:13 NLT
[5] Proverbs 16:3
[6] Psalm 57:2, 138:8 (See multiple translations of "performs.")
[7] John 14:6, 8:32

LIE #5: I can choose without impacting others.

[1] 1 Corinthians 6:19-20
[2] Romans 12:1
[3] 2 Corinthians 5:21
[4] Romans 6:13
[5] Joni Lamb, *Surrender All*, Water Brook Press, 12265 Oracle
   Blvd., Suite 200, Colorado Springs, CO 80921, 2008, page 43.
[6] Matthew 12:44-45
[7] John 10:29

THE TRUTH: Jesus can free me from the lies.

[1] 2 Thessalonians 2:11
[2] Ephesians 4:26-27 KJV, NASB
[3] Nathan Daniel, *Freedom through Forgiveness*, Vision
   Publishing Services, 1115 D Street, Ramona, CA 92064; 2007, p.
   64-66. Email at: www.FreedomThroughForgivenessMinistries.com
[4] Revelation 12:10b AMP
[5] 1 John 2:1
[6] Matthew 6:15, Luke 6:37 AMP
[7] Ephesians 4:26-27 AMP
[8] Ron Hogue, "Breaking Covenant with the Enemy," April 5,
   2009, Restoration Church, 1350 W. Euless Blvd., Suite 90,
   Euless, TX 76040; Listen to sermons, or email at:
   www.restorationdfw.org
[9] Joshua 9 and 10
[10] Joshua 9:7, 14

THE TRUTH: Freedom can be permanent.

[1] John 8:36
[2] Proverbs 4:23
[3] Proverbs 3:5
[4] Hebrews 10:25

THE TRUTH: Bringing it all together.

[1] Proverbs 14:12, 16:25 NIV [brackets added]
[2] Romans 1:22 AMP [parentheses added]
[3] Proverbs 3:5-6 NASB

THE TRUTH: What does it mean to be "born again"?

[1] John 3:1-21 NIV
[2] Psalm 57:2, 138:8
[3] 1 Peter 5:7

ADDENDUM

[1] 1987 copyright with Mercy Publishing. All rights reserved. International copyright secured. Written by D. J. Butler

[2] 1998 Word Music / Integrity's Hosanna! Music / ASCAP / All rights reserved. Used by permission. Written by: Cloninger, Claire / Sadler, Gary; Lyrics © Warner/Chappell Music, Inc.

[3] 1998 Word Music / Integrity's Hosanna! Music / ASCAP / All rights reserved. Used by permission. Written by: Cloninger, Claire / Sadler, Gary; Lyrics © Warner/Chappell Music, Inc.

www.ingramcontent.com/pod-product-compliance
Lightning Source LLC
Chambersburg PA
CBHW052358060726
47592CB00019B/1526